THE EASY TIMES TABLE BOOK

W. FOULSHAM & CO. LTD.
Thames Valley Court, 183-187 Bath Road, Slough, Berks., England
NEW YORK   TORONTO   CAPE TOWN   SYDNEY

THE EASY TWO TIMES TABLE

To know all your tables
you need to learn only
the ones in the boxes-
those figures not in the boxes
are in fact merely
repeats.

$$1 \times 2 = 2$$

$$2 \times 2 = 4$$

$$3 \times 2 = 6$$

$$4 \times 2 = 8$$

$$5 \times 2 = 10$$

$$6 \times 2 = 12$$

$$7 \times 2 = 14$$

$$8 \times 2 = 16$$

$$9 \times 2 = 18$$

$$10 \times 2 = 20$$

$$11 \times 2 = 22$$

$$12 \times 2 = 24$$

THE EASY THREE TIMES TABLE

To know all your tables
you need to learn only
the ones in the boxes-
those figures not in the boxes
are in fact merely
repeats of earlier pages.

1	×	3	=	3
2	×	3	=	6
3	×	3	=	9
4	×	3	=	12
5	×	3	=	15
6	×	3	=	18
7	×	3	=	21
8	×	3	=	24
9	×	3	=	27
10	×	3	=	30
11	×	3	=	33
12	×	3	=	36

THE EASY FOUR TIMES TABLE

To know all your tables
you need to learn only
the ones in the boxes-
those figures not in the boxes
are in fact merely
repeats of earlier pages.

1	×	4	=	4
2	×	4	=	8
3	×	4	=	12
4	×	4	=	16
5	×	4	=	20
6	×	4	=	24
7	×	4	=	28
8	×	4	=	32
9	×	4	=	36
10	×	4	=	40
11	×	4	=	44
12	×	4	=	48

THE EASY FIVE TIMES TABLE

To know all your tables
you need to learn only
the ones in the boxes-
those figures not in the boxes
are in fact merely
repeats of earlier pages.

$$1 \times 5 = 5$$

$$2 \times 5 = 10$$

$$3 \times 5 = 15$$

$$4 \times 5 = 20$$

$$5 \times 5 = 25$$

$$6 \times 5 = 30$$

$$7 \times 5 = 35$$

$$8 \times 5 = 40$$

$$9 \times 5 = 45$$

$$10 \times 5 = 50$$

$$11 \times 5 = 55$$

$$12 \times 5 = 60$$

THE EASY SIX TIMES TABLE

To know all your tables
you need to learn only
the ones in the boxes-
those figures not in the boxes
are in fact merely
repeats of earlier pages.

1	×	6	=	6
2	×	6	=	12
3	×	6	=	18
4	×	6	=	24
5	×	6	=	30
6	×	6	=	36
7	×	6	=	42
8	×	6	=	48
9	×	6	=	54
10	×	6	=	60
11	×	6	=	66
12	×	6	=	72

THE EASY SEVEN TIMES TABLE

To know all your tables
you need to learn only
the ones in the boxes-
those figures not in the boxes
are in fact merely
repeats of earlier pages.

1	×	7	=	7
2	×	7	=	14
3	×	7	=	21
4	×	7	=	28
5	×	7	=	35
6	×	7	=	42
7	×	7	=	49
8	×	7	=	56
9	×	7	=	63
10	×	7	=	70
11	×	7	=	77
12	×	7	=	84

THE EASY EIGHT TIMES TABLE

To know all your tables
you need to learn only
the ones in the boxes-
those figures not in the boxes
are in fact merely
repeats of earlier pages.

1	×	8	=	8
2	×	8	=	16
3	×	8	=	24
4	×	8	=	32
5	×	8	=	40
6	×	8	=	48
7	×	8	=	56
8	×	8	=	64
9	×	8	=	72
10	×	8	=	80
11	×	8	=	88
12	×	8	=	96

THE EASY NINE TIMES TABLE

To know all your tables
you need to learn only
the ones in the boxes-
those figures not in the boxes
are in fact merely
repeats of earlier pages.

$$1 \times 9 = 9$$

$$2 \times 9 = 18$$

$$3 \times 9 = 27$$

$$4 \times 9 = 36$$

$$5 \times 9 = 45$$

$$6 \times 9 = 54$$

$$7 \times 9 = 63$$

$$8 \times 9 = 72$$

$$9 \times 9 = 81$$

$$10 \times 9 = 90$$

$$11 \times 9 = 99$$

$$12 \times 9 = 108$$

THE EASY TEN TIMES TABLE

To know all your tables
you need to learn only
the ones in the boxes-
those figures not in the boxes
are in fact merely
repeats of earlier pages.

$$1 \times 10 = 10$$

$$2 \times 10 = 20$$

$$3 \times 10 = 30$$

$$4 \times 10 = 40$$

$$5 \times 10 = 50$$

$$6 \times 10 = 60$$

$$7 \times 10 = 70$$

$$8 \times 10 = 80$$

$$9 \times 10 = 90$$

$$10 \times 10 = 100$$

$$11 \times 10 = 110$$

$$12 \times 10 = 120$$

THE EASY ELEVEN TIMES TABLE

To know all your tables
you need to learn only
the ones in the boxes-
those figures not in the boxes
are in fact merely
repeats of earlier pages.

$$1 \times 11 = 11$$

$$2 \times 11 = 22$$

$$3 \times 11 = 33$$

$$4 \times 11 = 44$$

$$5 \times 11 = 55$$

$$6 \times 11 = 66$$

$$7 \times 11 = 77$$

$$8 \times 11 = 88$$

$$9 \times 11 = 99$$

$$10 \times 11 = 110$$

$$11 \times 11 = 121$$

$$12 \times 11 = 132$$

THE EASY TWELVE TIMES TABLE

To know all your tables
you need to learn only
the ones in the boxes-
those figures not in the boxes
are in fact merely
repeats of earlier pages.

$$1 \times 12 = 12$$

$$2 \times 12 = 24$$

$$3 \times 12 = 36$$

$$4 \times 12 = 48$$

$$5 \times 12 = 60$$

$$6 \times 12 = 72$$

$$7 \times 12 = 84$$

$$8 \times 12 = 96$$

$$9 \times 12 = 108$$

$$10 \times 12 = 120$$

$$11 \times 12 = 132$$

$$12 \times 12 = 144$$

TESTING TIME

When you have learnt your 2, 3, 4 and 5 times table try answering the multiplication sums in Group A.
Then do Group B when you have learnt tables 6, 7, 8 and 9 and finally Group C for tables 10, 11 and 12.

Group A	Group B	Group C
2×6	6×9	10×7
3×7	7×2	11×3
4×4	8×6	12×2
5×10	9×4	12×7
2×9	6×7	10×2
3×3	7×3	11×5
4×5	8×8	12×8
5×6	9×7	11×12
2×11	6×12	12×3
3×9	7×8	10×10
4×7	8×9	11×6
5×12	9×5	12×9
2×12	6×3	11×10
3×4	7×9	12×6
4×2	8×4	10×12
5×8	9×11	11×11
2×7	6×4	11×8
3×2	7×12	12×12
4×11	8×11	10×4
5×3	9×12	12×11

When you think you know all your tables you can test yourself by working from left to right across the columns.

ISBN 978-0-572-00990-8